Creative Activities to Stimulate Children

In the Classroom
In the School
In the Community

(Original title: Creative Activities for the Gifted Child)

by LEE BENNETT HOPKINS &

ANNETTE FRANK SHAPIRO

SCHOLASTIC BOOK SERVICES

NEW YORK • TORONTO • LONDON • AUCKLAND • SYDNEY

Copyright © 1969 by Fearon Publishers/Lear Siegler, Inc. as CREATIVE ACTIVITIES FOR THE GIFTED CHILD. All rights reserved. This special edition is published by Scholastic Book Services, a division of Scholastic Magazines, Inc., by arrangement with Fearon Publishers, 2165 Park Boulevard, Palo Alto, California 94306.

2nd printing .... March 1971.

Printed in the U.S.A.

Preface

Children need an environment that recognizes their superior capacity for intellectual growth and one that allows them to proceed at a pace commensurate with their abilities. Because of increasing demands on her time, the teacher may not always be able to provide this type of stimulating environment for the children. *Creative Activities in the Classroom* helps the teacher with this predicament by suggesting more than one hundred enrichment ideas. Although students do need the teacher's guidance, most are capable of working more independently than they are often allowed to do in traditional classrooms. The suggestions in this book recognize this fact and allow for the widest possible range of individual responsibility.

The activities encompass all fields — art, science geography, social sciences, history, mathematics, political science, music, language arts, home economics, and physical education. The children have opportunities to develop in their own classroom — in the school and in the community. Many of the activities offer students the opportunity to work closely with their classmates or with younger children and will bring them satisfaction from the knowledge that they are helping others.

Curiosity is one great motivation for children; the need for achievement is another. We have tried to recognize and satisfy both needs when developing the activities in this book. It is our belief that if children are encouraged and motivated to discover, inquire, create, and lead, their peers and their teachers will benefit from the excitement of richer, more imaginative, and more stimulating programs. The students themselves will profit from the chance to expand their horizons beyond the confines of the regular classroom program.

From the children of today will come the artists, musicians, writers, scientists, doctors, political and industrial leaders, educators, lawyers, and craftsmen of tomorrow. All possible steps must be taken to increase the educational opportunities for children. Hopefully, this book will add one more step in that direction.

Lee Bennett Hopkins
Annette Frank Shapiro

Contents

In the Classroom

Animators may draw pictures and attach them to a stick or a string. Figures, cars, trucks, planes, or ships may be moved by the children in front of miniature painted scenery to enliven a story of a personal experience. The Animators may also put on animated short plays, or they might draw pictures representing characters in a story the class is reading and use the pictures to illustrate the story. A committee of children could develop an educational, animated show, possibly built around a favorite story, and put it on for classes of younger children.

The **Art Collator** can assemble and mark boxes of material suitable for collages, mobiles, murals, puppets, dioramas, and masks for class use. He might also arrange art media, such as finger paint, clay, colored chalk, charcoal, crayons, and paints so that classmates may have the opportunity to use them. A desk or table can be covered with oilcloth to serve as an art center. A clothesline and some clothespins can be provided to display finished products. The Art Collator may also stimulate creativity by making a bulletin board display about artists — their lives and work.

■

Classroom programs offer the child many opportunities as an **Artist.** He may become an etcher, craftsman, sketcher, painter, illustrator, water colorist, landscapist, designer, cartoonist, sculptor, or modelist. The finished works of the Artists may be part of a changing art exhibit in the room. Children might also share their "know-how" with their classmates by giving talks on techniques, and/or lives of great artists.

■

Children can become **Book Reviewers** in several ways. Often, advance copies of books (review copies) can be obtained free by writing to publishers. Reviews of these books can be posted on a bulletin board to stimulate interest in a variety of subjects. Copies of reviews can be sent to the publishers.

Sometimes books already established in the field of children's literature can be re-reviewed. Children can compare their reviews with professional ones. Newbery award-winning books can help to make this activity exciting. Some popular Newbery award books include:

1934 *Invincible Louisa*, Cornelia Meigs (Boston: Little, Brown Company)

1936 *Caddie Woodlawn*, Carol Ryrie Brink (New York: The Macmillan Company)

1941 *Call It Courage*, Armstrong Sperry (New York: The Macmillan Company)

1949 *King of the Wind*, Marguerite Henry (New York: Rand McNally & Co.)

1951 *Amos Fortune, Free Man*, Elizabeth Yates (New York: E. P. Dutton & Co., Inc.)

1961 *Island of Blue Dolphins*, Scott O'Dell (Boston: Houghton-Mifflin Company)

1963 *A Wrinkle in Time*, Madeleine L'Engle (New York: Farrar, Straus and Giroux, Inc.)

1968 *From the Mixed-up Files of Mrs. Basil E. Frankweiler*, E. L. Konigsburg (New York: Atheneum Publishers, Inc.)

When writing a review, the student may react to illustrations, content, and characters. Book Reviewers could be encouraged to read aloud parts of the books and/or their reviews to their classmates.

■

Interested children can become **Botanists** and can collect, label, and take care of plants, as well as share information with their classmates about the plants' natural habitat, weather requirements, and proper care. Botanists may also conduct a planting session and help their peers to plant flower seeds, potatoes, or fruit pits.

■

Children can become **Campaign Managers** for classroom government officials. They might plan television debates, public campaign meetings, radio speeches, and poster displays, and provide ballots for elections. Elections should be held several times during the school year so that many children can participate and feel a sense of responsibility.

In addition to classroom-centered activities, the Campaign Managers can actively take part in national, state, and local elections. Some children can be elected to represent the opposing candidates. After the class is divided into political parties, the children can peruse newspapers and magazines in order to provide their side with facts and pertinent information for the campaign. Letters can be written to the actual candidates telling them of classroom activities.

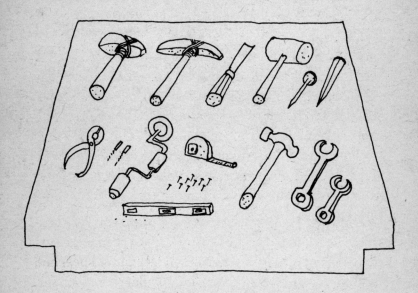

A child interested in tools and woodworking can become a **Class Carpenter**. He may collect samples of tools, demonstrate their proper use, and encourage an interested group to study the history of tools from those used by the caveman to those used by modern carpenters, mechanics, and metal workers of today.

An interested student may become the **Class Cartographer.** He can collect maps covering the following categories: physical features, political boundaries; locale of folklore and products; roads, weather, seas, streets, subways, and population.

After being labeled correctly for class use and discussion, these may be mounted in a large wall-chart book, or filed in a large carton. Children should be encouraged to use one type of map as a basis for a creative bulletin board display. For example, when using a neighborhood street map, strings may be connected to drawings or photographs of each child's house, labeled with his name, address, and zip code.

The Class Cartographer could learn about each type of map and report each day to his classmates about a different kind of map, explaining its meaning and purpose.

■

A committee of children can become **Class Curators** by collecting and organizing realia relating to the ongoing social studies unit. Toys and dolls of many lands; unusual household articles from foreign countries; books, newspapers, and magazines in foreign languages; and articles of clothing may be displayed, discussed, and used for dramatic play in a class "museum corner." The Class Curators can head a committee to paint and construct "museum" facades, murals, or dramatic play corners representing a western street scene, a Dutch fireplace, an Eskimo igloo, a Mexican adobe, or a Japanese teahouse. (A Japanese teahouse can easily be set up by placing bamboo poles

in flower pots or pails filled with earth or sand to act as supports for a paper pagoda roof. Inside, pillows on the floor, low tables, and Japanese tea sets can set the atmosphere for exciting dramatic play.)

Rows of seats can be utilized to dramatize a western town. The children in each row select a street name for their row, draw pertinent pictures, and don appropriate dress to represent different people in the town. Children should prepare talks or playlets illustrating their role in this society.

■

Mechanically minded children can become **Class Electricians.** They can set up and operate spotlights for dramatic programs, lights for shadow plays, or electrified boxes to display transparencies. They could set up a demonstration to show their classmates how the number of watts in a lightbulb relates to how bright the light is. The vast difference between a 25-watt bulb and a spotlight could be explained.

■

The **Class Interpreter** can make charts, wall-logs, and name cards of foreign words encountered in a social studies unit. He may label parts of the room, containers of food, or articles of clothing. This collection of words might start further research on a comparison of the word for any one article in different languages. For example, *book* is *livre* in French, *libro* in Spanish, and *hon* in Japanese.

∎

Class Librarians can teach the use of various reference books and materials. These might include almanacs, a thesaurus, encyclopedias, atlases, and/or the card catalog. More specific reference books, such as *Reader's Guide to Periodical Literature, Current Biography, Who's Who,* and *The Index to Children's Poetry,* may also be introduced by the Librarians.

∎

A group of students can be the **Classroom Publishers.** They can read and edit original stories, plays, and poems that have been submitted by classmates. If the material is "acceptable," they can negotiate contracts, select an illustrator, arrange for publicity, and set a publication date for the material. The Publishers may use the contributions to initiate a class literary review, a wall magazine, or to make a book for the class library. The selections may be sent to a school or local newspaper or to a national magazine for children.

Children can be **Cultural Chroniclers**, recording the history of the theater, dance, musical instruments, opera, architecture, and sporting events, such as the Olympic Games. These records may be written, painted, sculptured, constructed, or woven to enhance a chronological study of an area.

■

A few children might enjoy being **Current Events Reporters.** They can be responsible for a changing bulletin board on current events topics made up of newspaper and magazine clippings. They may gather pertinent background reading material and make it available to the class for research about the topics under consideration. Large envelopes tacked on the base of the current events bulletin board can hold literature related to the newspaper and magazine clippings. For example, if drought and forest fires are headlines in the news, pictures and reading matter on conservation will help the child understand the consequences of both.

Current Events Reporters can also make oral reports to the class about headlines and the stories behind them.

Children can become **Ecological Geographers.** Individuals or groups can study mountains around the world, desert areas, international water bodies, jungle lands, and arctic regions. They can prepare discussions on the effect that environment has had on mankind. The Geographers can enliven and clarify their discussions by preparing three-dimensional maps of clay, plasticene, plaster of Paris, or sawdust and paste to share with the class. Imaginary topographical maps may be made by using a sheet of drawing paper on which children begin by painting a river. Then, pieces of wet brown wrapping paper can be torn into strips and pinched up into mountain ranges, peaks, and plateaus. These may be added to the paper by using a thin layer of paste. Desert areas or fertile valleys may be painted in. These maps may be used to initiate thinking on the relation of people's work, homes, food, clothing, and transportation to the geographic area.

■

A **Flannel Board Artist** may make cut-outs to re-create story characters, places, and objects for dramatic presentations. The children may also be encouraged to create cut-outs to represent them-

selves, their family members, or fantastic animal creatures. They can weave stories around these cutouts as they move them on the flannel board.

■

Mathematically minded children can become **Geometry Consultants.** They can collect realia representing basic geometric forms; they can investigate and describe geometric forms used in the classroom, school, and in the community; they can collect literature related to geometry, such as the poems "Ring Around the World" or "Block City" from May Hill Arbuthnot's compilation *Time for Poetry* (New York: William R. Scott, Inc., 1961) or the book *A Kiss Is Round*, by Blossom Budney (New York: Lothrop Lee and Shepard, Co., Inc., 1954).

■

A committee of children may become **Grammarians** to discuss the proper use of tenses, parts of speech, punctuation, and diacritical markings. When written material is to be displayed and/or submitted for publication, this committee should assist in final corrections.

■

A very good student might become a **Hall of Fame Coordinator**. He may select topics and organize a committee to do the research and report on its findings. Some suggested topics include: composers through the ages, ethnic group personalities, folklore heroes, literature characters, American patriots, and modern-day inventors. Once the information has been gathered, it can be presented to the class in several ways. A bulletin board display can be created, including pictures of each hall of famer and a short biographical sketch. Oral reports could be given to the class. Each child could select a famous person to represent.

■

An interested student can become a **Historical Mathematician.** He can research any subject concerning mathematics from the history of math to the use of computers. For example, the child can trace the development of measuring devices, ways of telling time, ways of counting, and computing devices used from ancient to modern times and report his findings to the class. The student could make drawings to illustrate his report.

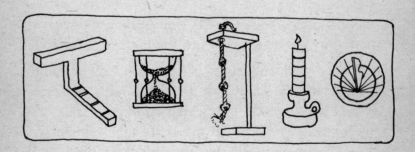

Holiday Historians can research origins and customs of holidays. They can make a comparison of how the same holiday is celebrated in different countries. They can collect ideas of crafts and recipes from popular family and teacher magazines, from parents and other adults. Wherever possible, samples should accompany the information to be shared. The Holiday Historians could plan a holiday celebration based upon the customs of one particular country.

■

An **Insect Zoologist** may set up a zoo in a science corner. Ants, beetles, crickets, and collections of butterflies and moths may be displayed. The Zoologist should be responsible for the care and feeding of the inhabitants in his zoo. He may enrich the science period by giving a talk about the life cycle, environmental requirements, etc., of one type of insect.

■

Even a young child may be an **Interviewer** and conduct interviews. Mothers may be asked for their favorite recipes; grandparents may be asked about their favorite childhood games; fathers could be asked about routes taken to and from work; older brothers and sisters could be asked about their favorite school subject; and storekeepers may be asked how foods are ordered, kept fresh, and weighed.

■

An interested student can be a **Junior Scientist**. He may:

1. Record ongoing science experiments in a class log.
2. Collect equipment for experimentation centering around a particular unit or theme.
3. Stimulate experiments by providing background material on scientists, inventors, and inventions.
4. Head a committee to do advanced science experiments and present the results to the class.
5. Be in charge of a bulletin board display to record experiments under such headings as: *What Am I Looking For? What Did I Do? How Did I Do It? What Did I Find?*

■

Each month the **Keeper of the Dates** can recognize important days. It will be fun to ferret out unusual dates throughout the school year. Information can be shared through artwork, informal dramatics, and written or oral reports. *History on Display,* by Katherine V. Bishop and Frank Follmer (Palo Alto, Calif.: Fearon Publishers, 1964) presents important moments in science, sports, the arts, and government in a series of full-color posters. Here is a sample of a few unusual dates for each month of the school year.

September

4 — In 1888 George Eastman patented the Kodak camera.

12 — In 1940 primitive drawings on cave walls were discovered at Lascaux, France.

23 — In 1846 the planet Neptune was discovered.

25 — In 1513 Balboa sighted the Pacific Ocean.

October

6 — In 1927 the first all-sound motion picture was shown. It was titled *The Jazz Singer* and starred Al Jolson.

8 — In 1871 the Great Chicago Fire began. It was rumored that it started because Mrs. O'Leary's cow kicked over a lantern.

13 — In 1754 Mary Ludwig Hays McCauley, better known as Molly Pitcher, was born.

23 — In 42 B.C. Brutus committed suicide.

November

3 — In 1900 the first automobile show opened in New York City.

6 — In 1905 Peter Pan was first performed in New York. The star was Maude Adams.

20 — In 1817 the Seminole Indian War began.

21 — In 1789 North Carolina became the twelfth state to ratify the Constitution.

December

6 — In 1884 the Washington Monument was completed.

12 — In 1901 Marconi's first radio signal was sent across the Atlantic Ocean.

19 — In 1732 Benjamin Franklin began publishing his famous *Poor Richard's Almanack*.

26 — In 1865 the first coffee percolator was patented by James Nason.

January

1 — In 45 B.C. the Julian calendar began.

7 — In 1610 Galileo discovered Jupiter's moons through his telescope.

23 — In 1888 The National Geographic Society was founded.

31 — In 1950 President Truman ordered the development of the hydrogen bomb.

February

8 — In 1587 Mary, Queen of Scots, was beheaded.
19 — In 1878 Edison was granted a patent for his phonograph machine.
23 — In 1861 Texas seceded from the Union.
28 — In 1820 Sir John Tenniel, illustrator of *Alice in Wonderland*, was born.

March

5 — In 1770 the Boston Massacre took place.
7 — In 1876 Alexander Graham Bell received a patent for his telephone.
25 — In 1871 Gutzon Borglum, American sculptor, was born. Mr. Borglum is famous for his carvings of Washington, Jefferson, Lincoln, and T. Roosevelt at Mount Rushmore.

April

7 — In 1614 El Greco, foremost painter of the Castilian school, died.
13 — In 1796 New York saw its first elephant.

18 — In 1906 San Francisco's earthquake occurred.

21 — In 753 B.C. Rome was founded.

May

7 — In 1915 a German submarine sank the *Lusitania*.

11 — In 1904 Salvador Dali was born. Mr. Dali, a leader of the surrealist school, is famous throughout the world for his paintings.

18 — In 1852 the state of Massachusetts passed the country's first compulsory school attendance law.

26 — In 1864 the Montana Territory was founded.

June

6 — In 1933 the first drive-in movie was opened.

8 — In 1869 the vacuum cleaner was patented.

11 — In 1965 Queen Elizabeth II made the Beatles members of the Order of the British Empire.

15 — In 1752 Benjamin Franklin flew a kite during a rainstorm to show that lightning was a form of electricity.

A student can become a **Language Etymologist** by tracing the origin of words and making a study of how a facet of language has changed to reflect the tempo of the times. The Language Etymologist can also build a word file of unusual adjectives, adverbs, and phrases, or compile lists of substitutes for over-worked words. *Roget's International Thesaurus,* 3rd ed. (New York: Thomas Y. Crowell Company, 1962) can supply exciting synonyms for "good," "adorable," "interesting," "pretty." He may use this file for his own creative writing and/or share it with classmates. He might also add definitions and diacritical markings for pronunciation use.

■

A child who can play a musical instrument can be a **Music Maker** and accompany class programs, reading of poetry, or choral speaking. He may head a committee of "musicians" who can produce sound effects, collect records, and compile a resource file of musical terms and/or musicians through the ages.

■

Original Storymakers can write satires, parodies, tall tales, or short stories in prose or poetry. Then the students can read or act out their stories. Class discussions and experiences, fairy tales, television programs, or popular movies can suggest content for these stories. Some titles might be:"If Mary Poppins Met Superman"; "Prehistoric Man Gets Lost in Space"; "If the Shoe Hadn't Fit Cinderella."

■

There can be **Pet Experts** in any class where there are fish, hamsters, turtles, frogs, etc. These students can set up a library corner with reading material on the habitation, feeding, and proper care of class pets.

■

An interested child can be a **Philatelist** and collect stamps of all kinds. He can organize them on charts or in booklets in several categories: countries, famous people, sports, historical monuments, events, or flora and fauna. He might also work together with the Postal Authorities (page 34) and do research on the history of the United States postal system and the design, production, and cost of American postage.

■

A group of young children may serve as **Picture Clippers** and develop a file of pictures centering around specific themes: community helpers, city and country animals, government figures, science "helpers" in the home, or pictures to represent word families. Smaller pictures may also be collected for illustrating student-made dictionaries.

Children can become **Play Instructors** for both quiet and active games. In the classroom, they may teach their peers how to play chess, checkers, anagrams, Scrabble, and other board games. Outdoors, they might help their classmates learn the rules and develop more skill in baseball, football, basketball, handball, and volleyball. In the gymnasium, they may assist in setting up gym apparatus and in leading circle or tag games.

■

A student can be a **Please-Send-Me Editor.** He can write to industries, embassies, chambers of commerce, and other places for free material. (Many sources can be found in *Selected Free Materials for Classroom Teachers*, by Ruth Aubrey, published by Fearon Publishers.) The booklets, pamphlets, pictures, maps, etc., that are obtained should be made available for individual and group research. These may be organized in a research file either alphabetically or topically. Some headings might include: Historical Background, Geographic Orientation, Transportation and Communication, Far Away and Long Ago, People Around the World, Culture and Customs, Inventors and Inventions, and Products and Producers.

Children might creatively use the materials for opaque projector talks, for dramatics, or for illustrating reports, booklets, and charts.

A **Poem Selector** may collect and have ready appropriate poems for special days and events, weather changes, seasonal changes, and timely happenings. These may be posted on a "poem pole" to attract the children as they enter the room. There should be some time set aside each week for poems to be read aloud and shared.

Several anthologies that were published many years ago are still popular with children today:

Dunbar, Paul Lawrence. *The Complete Poems.* New York: Dodd, Mead & Co., 1913.

Milne, A. A. *Now We Are Six.* New York: E. P. Dutton & Co., Inc., 1927.

Richards, Laura E. *Tirra-Lirra.* Boston: Little, Brown and Company, 1932.

Rossetti, Christina Georgina. *Sing-Song.* New York: The Macmillan Company, 1924.

Other anthologies that may prove valuable include:

Ferris, Helen (selected by). *Favorite Poems Old and New.* New York: Doubleday & Company, Inc., 1957.

Lewis, Richard (collector). *Miracles.* New York: Simon and Schuster, Inc., 1966.

Sandburg, Carl. *Early Moon*. New York: Harcourt, Brace & World, Inc., 1958.

———. *Wind Song*. New York: Harcourt, Brace & World, Inc., 1960.

■

The child may become a **Poet Laureate** by writing, reading, and teaching verse. Verse forms could include the usual couplets, triplets, quatrains, limericks, or free verse. Unusual forms of verse might also be included.

Haiku

Haiku, which originated in ancient Japan, has become very popular in American schools because of its simplicity and form. Haiku contains seventeen syllables in three lines, 5-7-5 respectively, and refers in some way to the seasons or nature.

> The huge oak tree stands
> Like a loving, kind mother
> Welcoming the birds.

(Fourth grade child)

Cinquain

Cinquain is an American form of verse that was created by Adelaide Crapsey in the early 1900's.

Cinquain contains twenty-two syllables in five lines, 2-4-6-8-2 respectively. The cinquain can be about any subject.

> Oh dear—
> Where is my key
> Where, oh where is my key?
> I shall have to look for it now!
> Oh dear!
>
> (Fifth grade child)

Sijo

Sijo is a product of fourteenth-century Korea. It originated during the Yi Dynasty and has recently become popular in America. The sijo form consists of six lines with six to eight syllabes in each line.

> Slowly falls the soft, soft snow
> White as sugar, white as milk —
> White as lace and white as the foam
> On the ocean's billowy waves.
> Wash your face in it! Throw it!
> I love the snow, don't you?
>
> (Sixth grade child)

The above verse forms share some basic features:

1. They are all brief.

2. They are based on syllabication.
3. They do not need to rhyme.
4. They can express a great deal of feeling, emotion, and thought in a few words.

A class post office can be organized and managed by **Postal Authorities**. A simple post office can be set up using decorated shoe boxes or large juice cans as repositories for incoming mail. Each child should have one. The post office may also serve as a place where the teacher may return written work, mimeographed announcements may be left, children may exchange notes, or greeting cards for all occasions may be "mailed." In addition to organizing a class post office, the Postal Authorities may want to investigate the history of the U.S. postal system and report to the class.

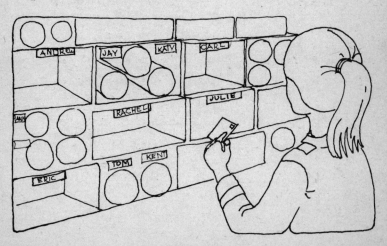

Roman Numeral Specialists can develop many interesting mathematical problems using Roman numerals. Perhaps they could dress in togas made from sheets to provide some atmosphere for the lesson. First they could teach the seven basic symbols, and then they could devise some activities. The basic symbols are:

I	V	X	L	C	D	M
1	5	10	50	100	500	1000

Here are suggested activities with Roman numerals:

1. See if you can turn the Roman numerals below into Arabic numerals.

   XXX _____   LVII _____

   VIII _____   CXXIV _____

   MDC _____   CCVII _____

2. See if you can write some numerals as Roman children wrote them:

   21 _____   29 _____

   4,900 _____   53 _____

   1,967 _____   1,492 _____

3. See if you can solve these problems:

Rose was born on the XVI day of the IV month in the year MCMLXVII. How many birthdays has she had? Peter lives at MCDXCII on XVI street. How far does he have to walk to XXIII street? to VIII street?

4. In what year did the following events occur:

a. Death of Abraham Lincoln — MDCCCLXV?
b. Death of John Kennedy — MCMLXIII?
c. Fall of Rome — CDLXXVI A.D.?
d. Beginning of World War II — MCMXXXIX?

■

An interested student can become a **Slide Etcher** and prepare original slides for "lectures." Lantern slides, 3¼″ x 4″, can be made of etched glass, clear glass, plastic, or cellophane. These slides can depict current units of study, such as Egyptian hieroglyphics, river patterns, mathematics formulae, parts of speech, and/or special hobbies and interests.

■

A child may become a **Social Secretary** of-the-week to make sure that a child who is ill receives a get-well note, study assignments, and reports of classroom activities.

A committee of talented children can become **Stagehands** to design and construct scenery and to collect and advise on properties needed for informal dramatics, formal dramatics, and dramatic play centers.

■

Statisticians can enrich the social studies program by acquiring a knowledge of comparative population figures, distances from place to place, land sizes around the world, transportation costs that vary according to the mode of travel, and temperature and rainfall figures. These may be recorded on graphs, compiled in a class book, used individually for an opaque projector, or drawn on transparencies for overhead projector demonstrations. Records might also be kept on batting averages, class averages, progress reports of campaigns, class attendance, and other topics of interest to the class.

■

Children with special skills can be **Student Consultants** to classmates and offer additional aid in sewing, constructing, reading, mathematics, spelling, etc. Notes might be posted on a bulletin board saying, "I can help today between 2:00 and 3:00 P.M.

in (area)." Children who wish help can sign up to use this consultation service.

■

A child can become a **Terminologist** and compile a class file of significant words and their meanings. Terminology for mathematics, science, political science, literature, etc. can be included. For example, a Science Terminologist can compile a list of scientific terms and their meanings. These may be recorded and illustrated on cards, and then placed in a file or booklet for class perusal. (Example: *Scuba diving* is a well-known term, but how many children know that the word *scuba* is derived from *s*elf-*c*ontained *u*nderwater *b*reathing *a*pparatus?)

■

Students can become **Time-line-ers** by researching and graphically recording information centered around a theme, such as Inventions, Explorations and Colonization, Art History, or The Negro in American History. Resulting time lines can be displayed in the classroom on a clothesline hanging across the room, on windows, poles, or the base of the chalkboard.

A study of the United States can be enriched by having children pose as **Town Criers** to research and "advertise" various topics including:

1. The natural wonders that attract tourists to various states.
2. The how, when, and why of place names on maps.
3. The legends and songs of America.

■

Vivid Inventors can develop ideas for inventions of the future. If possible, they might also make working models of their ideas. Sometimes they can be submitted for a contest; sometimes they may form an "Exhibit for the Year 2000"; often they will serve as a basis for science discussions. The following invention was designed by a sixth-grader:

Automatic Bedmaker

Just press the ON button and two arms will pick up the bed's blanket and shake it to make it easier to lay on the bed. Then, the other arm will pick up the pillow. Next, the arms will put down the blanket and smooth it out. Lastly, the pillow will come down on the bed.

A committee of **Who's Who Editors** can interview each child in the room for factual material that will be suitable for a biographical sketch. The Editors should decide upon information to be included and prepare a list of headings, such as name, address, family members, hobbies, pets, "favorites" (TV shows, books, movie stars, sports personalities), and future aspirations.

The Editors should give every child an opportunity to check his biography. In final form these biographical sketches can be bound in some way and can serve as reading material for the class or visitors to the classroom. The Who's Who booklets might be illustrated with original illustrations or photographs.

Word Experts can devise and mimeograph word games for individual or group use. These games may be used as part of the language arts programs before the regular school day begins or when work is completed. Time limits can add excitement to the games. Here are some examples that might be used to encourage children to produce their own games.

Fun with Initial Letters

Find a word beginning with each letter in each category.

	Cities	Mountains	Rivers	Famous Men	Products	States
A					Apple	
M			Missis-sippi			
E				Edison		
R	Roanoke					
I						Iowa
C		Catskill				
A				Attucks		

Finding Words Within a Word

Make as many words as you can out of the letters in the given word. For instance, there are at least 35 words that can be made out of *combination*.

Scramble Science

Unscramble the words listed below:

rcmosciepo	(microscope)
betu	(tube)
tmgaen	(magnet)
bblu	(bulb)
disesl	(slides)
ybrteta	(battery)
heccsalmi	(chemicals)

The **World Time Setter** can set a clock showing the time in any part of the world being studied in social studies. This could include the time belts in the United States or International Time Zones. Various discussions, led by the World Time Setter, can take place during the school day about what other people are doing in different parts of the world while the class is in session.

In the School

Alumni Detectives can locate and get in touch with people who have graduated from the school and have gone on to varied and unusual occupations and professions. Special assemblies could be planned to honor these graduates, who might talk to the students about their work. At other times a teacher may arrange for an interested child to make up and mail a questionnaire to graduates in a specific field of endeavor or to interview them personally. An annual ceremony can be planned and carried out by the Alumni Detectives to honor new inductees into the School Hall of Fame.

Animal Advisors may contact local zoos and arrange for live animals to visit the school. If a child has an unusual pet, the Advisor could arrange to have the pet brought to school. In preparation for the visit, the Advisor could publicize the event and prepare a talk about the animal-guest. Interested teachers may request this service.

A few children can become **Art Managers** and coordinate a changing exhibition of school art. The halls can become an art gallery with collections of work from all grade levels displayed. The exhibits could center around a specific theme decided upon by the committee or by a class. Themes might include: The City, Space, Illustrated Poems, Nature Collages, or Favorite Animals. Art Managers may also head a committee to collect reproductions of famous paintings. A file card should accompany each print, giving the title of the print, the artist's name, and some background information. This collection should be made available to classes throughout the school.

■

A group of children may become **Audiovisual Experts** by learning about and operating the various machines used in the school. These experts may also train children in other classes to use audiovisual aids. Children can be taught skills in running 16 mm. movie, slide, opaque, and overhead projectors, as well as tape recorders, cameras, microscopes, bioscopes, tachistoscopes, and Language Masters.

■

A committee of children can become **Bookstore Operators**. They may set up a school bookstore and sell paperback books and magazines. New stock may be purchased by this committee direct from publishers. A used-book section may also be added. This school service gives interested children opportunity to order books, sell and make change, account for sales, take inventories, aid in book selection for younger readers, review new selections, and survey popular selections and publish a "Best-seller List."

A few children may become **Costume Designers** for the school. They might:

1. Accumulate information on appropriate costumes for a period play and act as consultants to classes throughout the school.
2. Collect simple costume properties (hats, ties, scarfs, pocketbooks) and set up a prop-lending service.
3. Prepare costumes for play productions in the school.
4. Repair costumes so that they will be accessible for future productions.

■

Interested children can become **Culinary Artists** and assist teachers on days when cooking activities are in progress. They can often initiate the cooking experience by finding simple recipes for ice cream, cookies, gelatin salads, or candy.

■

Children enjoy being **Game Manufacturers**. They can make number and picture bingo games, matching word games, electrical quiz games, and map games. Games can be made from construction paper, large paper fasteners, envelopes, string, and pictures cut from magazines. The games can be distributed throughout the grades for additional activity in various curriculum areas. Here are some sample ideas:

1. Maps or pictures may be pasted on cardboard and cut to form pieces of a puzzle. After the puzzle is assembled by the child, questions may be posed on the puzzle's content.
2. "Plan-a-Trip" games can be made on any social studies topic. A map with fasteners and string should be part of the game so that children may plan "sight-seeing tours" on the map. Brochures and pamphlets obtained from travel agencies should be included so that information is available for planning the trip.
3. A science activity game on magnets may be developed. Such a game should include a magnet and three boxes: one labeled "Materials"; one labeled "Attracted"; and one labeled "Not Attracted." Children can be encouraged to detect the laws of magnetic behavior by experimenting with the magnet and materials provided (pins, paper, cloth, nails, iron, wood). A game of this type will involve children in meaningful experiences with magnets. "More-to-Do" cards could accompany the games to encourage further experimentation.

■

A committee of youngsters can be **Lenders of**

Science Kits. These experts can assemble the kits by collecting various materials, pictures, bulletins, and simple machines. Instructions for use should be included in each individual kit. This school service can be useful in stimulating group or class science activity. Topics may include: Kitchen Chemistry; Seeds for Planting; Sensory Materials for Sight, Sound, Smell, Touch, and Taste; and The Microscope: Slides and Materials for Looking.

■

Children can be **Library Assistants** and prepare posters to clarify a subject area of the Dewey decimal system used in libraries. Each poster might illustrate a topic under its proper number category. The Library Assistant can explain his poster to various classes to help other children achieve an understanding of the Dewey system.

■

Enterprising children can become **Museum Leaders.** Most museums throughout the country provide special educational programs for children. These programs are conducted on a class, small group, or individual basis. A Museum Leader can follow up on a museum trip in several ways:

1. He can conduct museum talks using realia or reproductions in the assembly or in a museum corner of the classroom.
2. He can develop fact sheets to describe the different exhibits of the museum and distribute them throughout the school.
3. He may map "trails" of the different halls to facilitate museum visits for others.
4. He may post bulletins announcing changing exhibits or new additions to museum collections.

■

Children interested in music can become **Musicologists**. They can prepare booklets highlighting songs and records to enrich any social studies unit. Topics may include Indian Rhythms; Songs of Colonial Days; Gay Nineties Tunes; Folk Songs Around the World; Work Songs; etc. They could also do some research on how music was copied years ago and how various instruments evolved. Perhaps an exhibit could be designed if some children have instruments or music that belonged to grandparents or great-grandparents.

As **Producer of the School Bulletin Board,** the child has the chance to create imaginative themes:

1. A school "newspaper," complete with headlines and featuring a social page, a sports page, a lost-and-found column, cartoons, and want-ads.
2. A map of the neighborhood showing recreational centers, historical landmarks, places of local interest, and unusual streets.
3. A "descriptive passage literary magazine" illustrating quotations, words, poems, thoughts, or images from favorite books.

■

Children can become **Puppeteers.** Puppets can be created from paper bags, socks, sticks, papier-mâché, cardboard, small boxes, or styrofoam. A puppet theater can be made, and plays can be written and produced using the children's puppet creations. These plays can be shown for assembly programs, at P.T.A. meetings, or to individual classes in the school.

■

Children can become **Radio Commentators** by using the school facilities to broadcast a variety of topics: outstanding events in the school; interesting neighborhood activities; advertisements or previews of books, movies, and television programs; customs of various holiday celebrations at appropriate times of the year; "feature stories" about personalities in the news; weekly reviews of the top news stories; and historical events told in a "You Are There" style.

A child can be a **Resource Cart Operator** and collect magazines, pamphlets, pictures, clippings, equipment, slides, and realia centering around a unit or theme. He can organize a cart to be rolled from room to room as an aid to motivating and enriching ongoing programs. Examples of rolling resource carts include:

The Traveling Mold Circus

Experiments on growing molds on different foodstuffs could be displayed and discussed with various classes.

A Country on Wheels

This cart can contain available materials for background and research on any country under current study.

Experiments with Magnets

An assortment of magnets is a must for this cart. Along with the magnets, varied materials to repel and attract plus related literature and pictures should be included.

Special Book Exhibit

A special book exhibit might concentrate on materials related to biography, autobiography, sports, poetry, plays, stories, or cater to individual interests.

The Hobby Wagon

This cart might display construction kits, sewing materials, art media, stamp collections, coin collections, puzzles and/or games, and the directions for their use.

■

Children can become **Roving Photographers** and offer their services to school personnel by snapping candid shots of children engaged in classroom or school activities. They may also photograph:

1. Children in front of their houses so that a teacher might use these snapshots on a "Who's Who?" bulletin board, a "Who Lives Where?" bulletin board, or a "Neighborhood Map."

2. School personalities and display them on a school bulletin board.

3. Office, custodial, cafeteria, teaching, and/or supervisory staff for a "Guess Who Gallery."

4. Visitors to the school — authors, school district personnel, entertainers, speakers, or community helpers. The photographs could be included in a *guest-book photo album*.

5. Special school events, bulletin boards, and art displays. These could be mounted into an annual school photo yearbook.

6. Various things of community interest, such as neighborhood buildings with unusual architectural or historical features, evidences of changing seasons, special neighborhood events, the local fireman, postman, sanitation collector, librarian, and corner policeman.

■

The **Social Studies Promoter** can create individual resource kits on places, people, and things around the world. These may be "advertised" from time to time and loaned to classes for enrichment. The kits can be made of cardboard boxes and can include a country's flag, an item of wearing apparel, a toy, a musical instrument, a book in a native language, and background information on the contents of the kit.

■

The child can become a **Student Teacher** by reading stories to children in lower grades. Several children can assist the Student Teacher by reading dialogue with him, by producing sound effects, and by acting out the story in dance or mime. Other children can prepare and show original illustrations, animated drawings, or puppets based on the story.

Sometimes original slides, transparencies, or pictures for the opaque projector can be produced for this school service. The reader may also dress in costume to represent a character in the story. Often original stories can be written and illustrated by the Student Teacher to be used as reading material.

■

Tape Technicians can perform a school service to teachers by using the tape recorder to record choral speaking, group singing, panel discussions, assembly plays, classroom dramatics, and instrumental music. These tapes may be played back to individual classes so that the children hear themselves as others hear them. Tape Technicians can also tape sounds in the neighborhood — rain falling on a roof, traffic noises, running water, or the cacophony of machines used in various construction projects. These tapes can be filed and used for science discussions, creative writing experiences, or as background sound effects for dramatic presentations.

■

Children can be **Thought-Provokers** by setting up school contests with questions and activities such as:

1. How many beans are in the jar?

2. Who is the Mystery Guest? (A picture of a famous personality can be shown.)
3. Solve the science formula.
4. What building is this? (A picture of a famous landmark can be posted.)
5. Where does this take place? (A picture of an event, a particular location, or a situation can be posted.)

A ballot box should be provided for the answers, and some provisions made for recognition of winners.

■

Tourist Consultants can run a travel bureau and specialize in planning "trip-tix." These trip-tix may be based upon requests from teachers who want to "plan a trip" in relation to a specific social studies area. Mileage, travel routes, temperature changes, time belts, suggested places to stay, and things to see can be included.

■

An interested child may become a **Travel Lecturer** and lecture to various grades about anything — from the immediate community to world communities. For example, a child may become so knowledgeable

about Indian life and culture in the United States that he will be able to enrich the curriculum in grades where this is a unit of study. Another child might be interested in contributions made by minority cultures in the United States and lecture to classes where this information would be applicable. Children who have the opportunity to travel to islands, other countries, or to places in the United States may be encouraged to keep travel diaries and to collect realia and printed material. These personal experiences can be the basis of exciting travelogues.

Young Biographers in the upper elementary grades can collect data in response to requests from other classes in the school. Second, third, or fourth graders can write letters to the fifth and sixth graders about any well-known person who interests them, asking for additional biographical information. In answer to individual or group requests, Young Biographers may prepare booklets, reports, or picture stories. In cases where an entire class is interested in a famous personality, broadcasts, panel discussions, "lectures," or readings may be prepared.

In the Community

An **Art Sponsor** can arrange for local stores, banks, and libraries to exhibit children's artwork. He might also plan an annual sidewalk or schoolyard art show. People in the community, as well as the children, might be invited to exhibit their art.

■

Children can be **Block Party Consultants** and collect songs, dances, stories, and the history of contributions made by ethnic groups represented in the community. These Consultants might initiate a block party to highlight the varied cultural gifts.

Collectors for Charity can head committees to collect and mend books, magazines, toys, and games for distribution through local agencies.

■

A committee of students can become **Community Investigators** to assess the problems of traffic conditions. Suggestions for improving conditions may be forwarded to local city councils. Some of the problems needing study might include corners where lights and/or traffic police are needed badly, streets in need of repair to facilitate transportation, and places where traffic signs are needed.

■

Community Liaison Personnel can recommend neighborhood personalities for a Community Hall of Fame. Stories written by the children about the people chosen can be featured in school or local newspapers. In addition, the Community Liaison Personnel can keep a record of community events that would interest their classmates, attend these events, and report on them. A list of interesting events, including times and places, could also be posted on the school bulletin board.

Children can become **Deputies for Cleaner Communities.** They can make anti-litter posters to be displayed in neighborhood stores to encourage everyone to work for a cleaner neighborhood. They might write to the local sanitation department to request the placement of additional litter cans and more frequent refuse collections. Anti-litter literature might be distributed by the Deputies in the school and community.

■

A committee of **Historians** can investigate the history of their community. Individual or group stories may be written, or a portfolio of photographs can be compiled to become part of the school or community library. The Historians might wish to give an illustrated talk on the community's history before the school assembly or in individual classrooms.

■

A **Horticulturist** might contact local florists or nurseries for a donation of shrubs, plants, or trees to the school to celebrate special events, holidays, or especially, Arbor Day. Plant life on school grounds might be dedicated to an outstanding personality in the community. A committee might work with the Horticulturist in preparing a dedication program involving the school and community officials. The foliage might be changed seasonally with running commentaries given over the school broadcast system, in the school newspaper, or on bulletin boards, to explain the various types currently on display.

■

A **Library Promoter** may encourage more use of the local library. He might:

1. Interview the librarian or other library personnel for the school newspaper.

2. Publicize special exhibits and special events about to take place at the library.

3. Describe the varied facilities, working together with the Library Assistants and the Class Librarian.

4. Arrange a tour through the local library and point out ways in which the school and local libraries are similar.

5. Help to "advertise" new books, old favorites, magazines, and recordings.

A group of children can become **Neighborhood Surveyors**. They can plan a series of walking tours for many purposes:

1. To map the immediate neighborhood.
2. To observe city, state, and federal government at work.
3. To see language usage, such as abbreviations, parts of speech, numbers.
4. To note signs of communication forms through language, science, and inventions.
5. To view historical buildings, streets, homes, landmarks, and architectural design.
6. To spot early evidence of seasonal change.

■

An **Observation Stimulator** can conduct "on-the-spot" quizzes of his classmates to sharpen their powers of observation. The content of the questions may be derived from the community:

1. Name the variety of manhole covers on our school block.
2. What types of fire hydrants are used in the community?
3. On what corners are streetlights placed?
4. What are the colors of the various traffic signs,

e.g., the stop sign, school crossing sign, rail-road crossing sign, no parking sign?

5. What types of buiding materials are used in surrounding buildings?

Questions also may be based on observations in the school:

1. How many exits are there?
2. How many classrooms?
3. What types of machines are used in the school office?
4. Name the types of personnel in the school.

■

A child can become a **Program Producer** and set up assembly programs involving people in the community who are available for speaking engagements in the school. A parent, a local storekeeper, the neighborhood policeman, a banker, a government official, or a travel agent is often happy to participate in school functions. (He might also work with the Alumni Detective to bring graduates to the assembly.)

■

A committee of children can become **Recreation Officers** to investigate available community-sponsored programs for young people. These might include Little League teams, after-school centers, summer or winter recreational facilities, and special library events. Recreation Officers can also assess available play areas and, through local agencies, work for additional cleared lots, play streets, and playgrounds.

■

The community offers the opportunity for the child to develop into a **Science Specialist.** He may be a liaison between local Audubon clubs, gardening clubs, conservation groups, etc., and the school. He could plan and lead field trips to share his knowledge with others.

■

A committee of children can become **Trip Consultants** by investigating the neighborhood and preparing a trip directory for the use of the school. This directory might include:

1. The geography, flora, and fauna of the community.
2. Services for health, protection, and recreation.
3. Transportation and communication facilities.
4. Past and present history of the community.
5. Neighborhood demolition and construction.

6. Unusual architecture, with an emphasis on foreign origin.
7. Names and locations of stores that sell, repair, and service commodities. (The Trip Consultants can work closely with the Neighborhood Surveyors in this activity.)

■

Want-ad Editors could contact people in the community who might need after-school workers throughout the year. Notices about jobs — mowing lawns, shoveling snow, walking dogs, raking leaves, delivering packages, and baby-sitting — may be posted by the Editors on a prominent bulletin board or announced over the school's public address system. The Want-ad Editors may also run a "For Sale" service, offering used books, toys, and games.

Ambassadors-at-Large

International understanding can be fostered in the classroom, school, and community by Ambassadors-at-Large through a variety of activities.

Interested children can act as **African Historians** and, using a changing map of Africa, trace the history of the continent, the formation of new, independent countries, and the organization of African unity. This information may be the basis for round-table discussions comparing Africa's present-day problems with those of the United States in its early days.

Since items of wearing apparel reflect both time and place, an international boutique might be set up by **Apparel Researchers** to display the history of clothing. A special art exhibit might focus on "Shoes Through the Ages" from the Roman cothurnus (A.D. 100) to modern footwear worn in the United States today.

∎

An exchange of artwork can be encouraged by **Exchange Ambassadors** when they collect and distribute media to children of other lands. One kit might include boxes of crayons and sample work done by students showing the many varied techniques using crayons. A letter should accompany the kit asking the students of another country to send a kit in return with samples and explanations of their techniques. The same may be done with colored chalk, charcoal, or materials for collages.

∎

Children may be encouraged to learn about foods of other lands by visiting local stores or gourmet shops. Tasting parties may be planned by the **Food Ambassadors** featuring an assortment of foods from any one country or highlighting one food under a heading, such as "Soups Around the World" (minestrone, Italy; won ton, China; scotch broth, Scotland) or "Cheeses Around the World" (provolone, Italy; Edam, Holland; bleu, Denmark).

■

Goodwill Ambassadors may pack and mail goodwill boxes to children in deprived areas of the United States as well as throughout the world. Each box might have a theme: Health Necessities; Holiday Customs; Local Environment Artifacts; Used Book Exchange; etc. The Goodwill Ambassadors can have the responsibility for correspondence to locate a needy child, either in the U.S. or another country.

■

A committee of **Greeting Card Artists** can be appointed and given the responsibility of acknowledging holidays. Original greeting cards can be hand drawn or printed. Materials for the cards can be gathered from art books, travel brochures, children's literature, and field trips. These cards may be sent on appropriate holidays to members of the armed forces, Peace Corps, health services, and/or international pen pals.

Interested children can become **International Bankers.** They can collect and display foreign money — *lire* from Italy, *pesetas* from Spain, *yen* from Japan, *dollars* from Hong Kong, *guilders* from Holland, *shillings* from England, *francs* from France, and *krone* from Denmark. Conversion tables may be obtained from airlines or travel bureaus and used to enrich mathematical discussions. Children can have practical experience with foreign money exchange by purchasing articles in a class international boutique or a world's fair.

■

International Biographers can maintain a bulletin board and feature current world leaders in the news. The children can write short biographical sketches and keep a log of activities engaged in by each personality. This activity can encourage debates, broadcasts, and panel discussions. In addition, there could be a bulletin board display of international writers and illustrators of children's books featuring a world map, pictures, book jackets, and biographical sketches of the illustrators. Some suggested personalities might include John Tenniel (*Alice in Wonderland*), Miroslav Sasek (*This Is . . . Series*), Claire Huchet Bishop (*Twenty and Ten*, Scholastic edition:

The Secret Cave), Rumer Godden *(Little Plum)*, Eric Kastner *(Emil and the Detectives)*, Astrid Lindgren *(Pippi Longstocking)*.

■

Interested children can be **International Musicologists** and do research on music, musical instruments, and composers of other lands. They can plan an international music festival that may highlight live or recorded programs centered around a theme: "Music of the Seasons"; "Primitive Rhythms"; "Music Tempos of the Times"; etc. The International Musicologists might also do research to learn about dances of other countries and the music to which the dances are performed. Then they might wish to plan a folk ballet featuring dances from around the world. They may demonstrate the dances and teach them to other students, collect appropriate music, and assist in the preparation of costumes and scenery.

■

An enterprising child may serve as **International Pen Pal Organizer** and write to tourist information bureaus or departments of education in any city of the world to obtain addresses of children and schools for an interchange of letters.

International Toy Specialists can set up a shop to display and/or sell toys, dolls, puppets, and games. These items could have been received in exchanges made with various countries. The children can often create replicas of various items from other countries after researching costumes, folklore, and culture.

■

Children can be **Lexicographers** and compile vestpocket dictionaries made up of lists of common English words and their equivalents in foreign languages. The dictionaries may also include sections on similarities and differences among names in various countries (Jean, Jan, John; Mary, Marie, Maria), derivations of place names in the United States (Baton Rouge, New York, Los Angeles), and words used internationally (chaffeur, pizza, plaza).

■

Starting in the home, children can be **Material Detectives** and look for international raw materials that are used for the necessities of life, artistic endeavors, and personal adornments. Mother-of-pearl from Japan, rubber from Brazil, industrial diamonds from South Africa, and nickel and copper from Chile are several of the important materials that are frequently used.

■

Service Publicists can contact organizations, such as the Red Cross, the United Nations in New York City, and the Peace Corps in Washington, D.C., to obtain information about their services and ways in which local participation can be encouraged.

As **Symbol Historians,** children can peruse advertisements, commercial brochures, television programs, newspapers, and magazines to discover unusual symbols that are used in industry. The Symbol Historian can do research to discover the origins of these symbols. Bookmarks can be made showing the origins (Mercury, used by florists and telegraph companies; Pegasus, used by a gasoline firm, etc.). Textile designs may be created reflecting the motifs, colors, shapes, and symbols that depict various world cultures: fleur-de-lis from France, shields and coats-of-arms from England, or religious artifacts from Africa.

■

The United Nations can be a rich source for many varied activities organized by a **U.N. Delegate.**

1. Mock U.N. sessions may be planned. "Delegates" from many nations can present and debate contemporary issues of world importance.
2. Flags of the U.N. may be made or drawn and displayed.
3. Card files of terms used in the U.N. may be compiled.
4. Biographical sketches of outstanding personalities connected with the U.N. can be prepared. Personalities might include Eleanor Roosevelt, Ralph Bunche, Dag Hammarskjöld, and U Thant.

5. Information can be gathered and shared about each of the U.N.'s main organs and its service organizations. Posters can be made to represent each branch of the U.N.
6. A time line can be constructed to depict chronological efforts toward world peace. An accompanying outline map can be used to show the locations of peace conferences around the world.
7. U.N. bibliographies of books, films, and filmstrips can be compiled for school or classroom libraries.
8. Articles about U.N. activities may be culled from several different newspapers. These articles may be the basis of discussions as to how various newspapers reflect points of view.
9. Three-dimensional maps can be made to show places in the world that have insufficient resources and are receiving aid from U.N. agencies.

■

Unusual Fact Researchers can collect information relating to transportation around the world. They might find out how people carry children, packages, household articles, clothing bundles, and water in the U.S. and various other countries now and long ago.

Further research may answer additional questions such as:

1. What animals are used as beasts of burden in countries or land regions around the world?
2. What influence has the invention of the wheel had on man's environment throughout history?

Index